TESTIMONIALS

The Earning Advantage is ideal for helping people understand how to love their jobs, become invaluable, and make more money.

—Gino Wickman
Author of *Traction* and Creator of EOS®

As a business owner, I want my employees to succeed! *The Earning Advantage* gives them a roadmap to exponential success! It's a tool to take the mystery out of how to be a great employee and how to make bosses love having you on the team. My advice to all employees: read *The Earning Advantage*. Then, take responsibility for your career by following this road map. You can do this! Jill has shown you how.

—Ronald A. Pyke, CPA CFO,
President of vbo Solutions

Jill Young lays it out in *The Earning Advantage*. Essentially, Jill says, 'here are the plays, this is how you will be measured, work hard, contribute as a team member, help us win, *then* ask if you have earned it.' This is a great book to give to teammates when they are confused about productive value and entitlement.

—Walt Brown, Business Owner
Coach and World-Class EOS Implementer since 2008

The Earning Advantage gets to the essence of what it takes to get ahead and stay ahead. Jill's method arms team members with simple tools that will inspire them to abandon the thought that the key to success lies with anyone other than themselves. Jill's writing style is fun and approachable and keeps the reader glued. Great bosses will hand these books out like candy!

—Alex Freytag, Certified EOS Implementer
Author, Entrepreneur, Integrator at ProfitWorks LLC

Jill 'knows' people and business requirements like no one else. In *The Earning Advantage*, she cuts to the quick and shows employees how to improve themselves and their workplaces. Jill is the Vince Lombardi of business coaches: 'If Jill tells you to go to hell, you look forward to the trip!'"

—Rick Pietrykowski, President of Surface Armor LLC

Finally, Jill has put into words what I have been trying to get across to team members for years…a definite proven process.

—Roger Sage, Owner of Baxter Sales

As a supervisor or manager, I would definitely give *The Earning Advantage* to employees. This book can help you determine if you are qualified to ask for a raise and explains ways we can all improve and prove it before assuming we are worth more. I like how the book makes you accountable to earn the raise you are seeking.

—Jessica Glover

This book is for the employees who are willing to go the extra mile. It's for the employees who can show their company that they are truly invested in its growth and success, and theirs! Jill points out that true team-players understand the direct correlation between their company's profitability and their own success. The tools introduced in this book are excellent exercises to improve employee awareness, efficiency, and productivity.

—Elinor Rowan

After reading *The Earning Advantage*, I know what kind of employee I want to be and where I need improvement. I walked away with a better ability to self-reflect that I didn't have when I started the book.

—Ashley Germany, CPA

Other Books by Jill Young

*The Courage Advantage: 3 Mindsets Your Team Needs to
Cultivate Fierce Discipline, Incredible Fun,
and a Culture of Experimentation*

*The Thinking Advantage: 4 Essential Steps Your Team
Needs to Cultivate Collaboration, Leverage Creative
Problem-Solving, and Enjoy Exponential Growth*

The
Earning
Advantage

8 Tools You Need to Get Paid
the Money You Want

Second Edition

JILL YOUNG

Published by Author Academy Elite
PO Box 43, Powell, OH 43065
www.AuthorAcademyElite.com

First edition published December 28, 2016.

Library of Congress Control Number: 2020908716

Softcover: 978-1-64746-275-8
Hardcover: 978-1-64746-276-5
E-book: 978-1-64746-277-2

Also available on audiobook.

To my parents,
Darlene and Gary,
who taught me to work hard by example
and encouraging words.

CONTENTS

INTRODUCTION

This is your step-by-step how-to guide to impact your company's bottom line, and yours! And don't freak out—earning more money is going to be hard work, but you're about to learn tools that will earn you more money forever.

YOU ARE HERE! BUT WHY?

You were just given this book because you asked your boss for a raise.

Congratulations! Your boss believes you've got the right stuff to make it in this company! Reading this book is your first step to getting the raise you want. Hopefully, he or she used this phrase:

I appreciate your desire for growth; please read this book, and schedule a time to talk with me in a few weeks.

Or: Maybe you went on the hunt for a book like this and purchased it on your own. Thanks! You are already 95% ahead of the rest of the workforce that will wait to be *given* a raise.

Or: Maybe you received this as a gift from someone who believes that you can create a better future for yourself. Thank them, humble yourself, and dig in.

In any case, I'm personally excited to help you, and I want you to be successful! But you need to want it more than I do...

HOW TO GET THE MOST OUT OF THIS BOOK

1. Be open. Be open to new ideas, trying things again, and using all of the tools I'm going to teach you.

2. Work for long-term gain; successful people delay gratification. These tools will take time and dedication. They will work if *you* work! This method is based on true, proven principles, nothing fancy, tricky, or misleading because I want you to be successful forever—not just today. All lasting strategies start on the inside and work their way to the outside.

3. Just start. The first steps in this process might feel a bit scary or uncomfortable. *Nothing great was ever achieved without a little trust and guts!* But don't wait. Start right now; you'll thank me later!

4. Be honest and bold. I'm going to ask you to be honest with yourself. I'm going to ask you to answer hard questions. Taking an honest look at yourself and your behaviors now will help you get to where you want to be. If you are less than truthful with yourself, you will end up where someone else wants you to be.

WHEN THIS WON'T WORK

Yep, I'm saying that there is a chance that this journey we are about to go on might not work. Here are some reasons why that could happen.

1. If you don't work for a human. If you work for a robot or a dictator, this might not work. I'm assuming that you work for reasonable, rational humans like the hundreds of bosses I've worked with over the last few decades.

2. If you don't love your job. Love is a strong word…I'll settle for *like*. But if you really hate your job, this is going to be a nightmare. So, I'm assuming that you at least like your job and the company you work for. Cool?

HOW TO READ THIS BOOK

1. Take a look at the Scorecard on the following pages. Go ahead and rank yourself as you are today. After you've worked with the tools for a while, go back and rank yourself again to see how far you've come.

2. Read this book from cover to cover. Get all the tools in your head without doing the exercises.

3. Then, read it again while doing the exercises. I strongly urge you to either write directly in the book (make it your own) or download the workbook at JillYoung.com. You'll come back to it often throughout your career, and it will be inspiring to see your notes. If you just can't write in a book (because your third-grade teacher threatened you with your life!), use a separate notebook of your own to keep track of your notes.

4. Next, as you work through the steps, come back to the book often for inspiration and direction.

5. Share it. If this book and the tools within work for you, tell your co-workers, friends, and teenagers about to enter the workforce about the book. Together, we'll introduce the world to these amazing tools!

The Earning Mindset SCORECARD
for use with *The Earning Advantage* by Jill Young

STATEMENTS	1 – 3	4 – 6	7 – 9	10 – 12	Score	Goal
I take responsibility for my own money-making abilities.	I only do what I'm told to do and if asked to do more, will do so only if I'm rewarded immediately (with overtime, an extra day off, etc.). If I wait long enough and keep working hard, someone will notice my efforts and reward me with a raise.	I'll do extra if asked but will make my boss feel that I'm really doing him/her a favor. I say things like, "Remember this when it's time for a raise?" I sometimes say, "If I got paid more I would be willing to do more."	I regularly volunteer to take on extra projects or assignments when asked and am happy to do so. However, I am uncomfortable asking my boss for a raise. I'll get a raise when my boss feels that I've earned it.	My boss knows (because we've had a conversation about it) that I want to earn more money by producing more value. I ask for challenging projects or assignments that will help build my productivity and value to the company.		
I produce value in my job.	I make lots of mistakes that other people need to clean up. I am one of the lower producers in my group. When my boss talks to me, he/she is mostly encouraging or teaching me ways to only do the job that was asked of me.	I get my regular job done before it's time to go home for the day, but I find that sometimes I have to do it over again. When my boss talks to me, he/she wants me to do more of what I'm doing but not spend as much time on it. He/she would like me to work faster, with a higher quality of work.	I get a lot done and in less time than my peers. My work is always at or above standard. My boss often praises my work. When people talk about me, I can hear them saying, "I don't know how **** does it, but he's/she's amazing at his/her job."	I am a high producer. I have worked hard to figure out how to do my job with the highest quality in the least amount of time. I look for opportunities to train others. When people talk about me, I can hear them saying, "He is the best**** we have."		
I see the big picture of what my company is doing.	When I come to work, I am focused on getting my job done. I rarely think about (or research) how my job affects other departments or what the company's goals are. When I do think about it, it's because my boss or someone else has brought it up in conversation or in company/department meetings.	Occasionally, I have thoughts about how what I do is important to the whole company, but only when prompted. If another department suggests or requests something of me, it is a nuisance, but I comply, sometimes adding my complaint of "why?" or "that's ridiculous" or "a waste of my time."	I'm excited to see our product/service in the marketplace. I frequently engage in conversations with others outside my department. I've been to the company website and I know how we sell our product/service. I have a good idea of what is important to our customer, and I'm excited about my part in the company.	I know the big picture of the company because I have had conversations with my boss or others in the company about short- and long-term goals. I keep up with our industry and where it's going. I align my actions with the goals of the company and give regular feedback about how the company could get closer to our goals by solving problems in my department.		
I have good work habits.	I occasionally take unscheduled days off if I don't feel good or just need to take a day for myself. I push the limit when it comes to being late, but as long as no one complains, it's fine. I sometimes forget to do tasks and need to be reminded or motivated by my boss or coworkers. When I enjoy participating in the company gossip, often complaining about company events or policies. When I violate company policy, I figure it doesn't matter unless someone says something to me.	I'm mostly on time and rarely take unscheduled days off. I'm pretty good about complying with company policies, although I might complain about it to others. I'm pretty pleasant to work with and cooperate with my coworkers. When it comes to issues within the company, I can be negative or positive, changing my attitude with the situation. I can be known to side with the situation. to. Every once in a while, I miss deadlines, but it's rarely my fault when I do.	I have a positive attitude about work and my position. I can be counted on to be on time and work a full day with focused effort. If a situation arises, I can see both sides of the issue but push through with a "can-do" attitude. If I miss a deadline or don't follow through on a promise, I admit it and try to fix it. I'm rarely late for work. I often stay late to finish projects or follow through on promises. I get it done, and people know they can count on me.	I am early or on time for work each day. My positive approach to solving problems has an effect on others in my department. When I don't feel like working, I come to work anyway pushing through like a champ. I manage my time well, keep my promises, and get everything done while leaving time to plan the next day. I don't participate in company gossip, only issue-solving sessions. I've made keeping company policies a part of my routine, so they don't interrupt my productivity.		

I have productive conversations with my boss.	My boss has enough to do. I only initiate a conversation with him or her when there is something wrong or when I need something.	My boss is pretty cool and we talk about lots of different topics. I feel that I can trust him/her. If there is something that needs to improve about my performance, he/she will bring it up. I'm sure I don't think he/she would be comfortable talking about how I could earn more money with the company.	I talk with my boss regularly about things that are important to the department. He/she values my opinion and often asks how I think we could improve the company. My boss has mentioned that he/she'd like to promote me someday, usually during scheduled performance reviews.	I've had a productive conversation with my boss about how I can earn more money within the company. I not only point out issues, but I also share ideas about how the issues can be solved. My boss and I have a "game plan" for how he/she is coaching me to be more valuable to the company. Often, I am the one asking for the appointment on my boss's calendar.
I solve problems to help the company.	I can see a lot of ways that the company or my department could improve, but I'm sure my boss sees it too. He/she does not want me to "rub it in" by bringing it up over and over again. It's good enough. This is the way things have always been done.	Occasionally, I complain or mention that things could be done differently, but I don't pursue the topic when no one wants to listen. My coworkers see it too, and we talk about it often, but rarely make any suggestions of how to solve the issue.	When I see something that could be improved, I make a comment to my boss. If he/she asks for suggestions for improving it, I'll spend a few minutes thinking about it but then get back to work. The problem only comes up again the next time I think about a particular issue.	When I find a problem in the department, I schedule a time to talk to my boss about it. Before the meeting, I spend a few hours thinking through possible causes and solutions. I offer to do additional research toward a solution. Afterward, I look for a next step to finding a solution.
I serve others around me so that they produce value.	I only help other people when they ask me to. When they ask, I will help them, but on my timeline. If it's not convenient for me, they are going to need to wait until I have time for them.	I help others when they ask me to help, but most of the time, I just end up doing the task for them. It's easier to do it myself than to teach someone else how to do it. They are mostly appreciative, but when I help, I often feel like I'm being taken advantage of.	I can be heard saying, "If you need any help at all, please ask me." When I help people, I like to show them how to do it. When they watch me do it, they learn faster. I like that people depend on me, and it is a big compliment when they ask for help.	I look for opportunities to teach others what I know. I'm willing to invest time in other people. I don't rescue people by telling them exactly what to do. I ask them questions that get them to think. Lots of people whom I have helped have gone on to help others.

WE CAN DO THIS!

Why do I say *we*? Because *we* are in this together: you and I, two people who have a part in building our ever-growing country. I'm an obsessive optimist, and I believe that right now, 300 million people are building our country in 300 million different ways. Getting right down to the basic fundamental building blocks of our country means that we start by building up individual people.

Can you be selfish for a minute?

Selfish is not a word most advisors will tell you to be, but I will. Selfish, but with a new definition: selfish means that you take care of yourself, that you start with yourself, that you focus on yourself, that you pay attention to yourself and your needs, and that you invest in yourself. Think about it as putting on your oxygen mask before you help others put on theirs. Think about it as mastering a task so you can then teach others.

So, can you be selfish?

I hope so, because your company needs you to be selfish, your family needs you to be selfish, your country needs you to be selfish, and I need you to be selfish because this book is going to require you to be selfish.

And you won't be alone!

We are on the same team, you and me. I'm on your team, and you're on mine. We need each other. I'm on a quest to move companies forward and inspire people to create great lives for themselves. You have your purpose, and I'll bet you need money (as a tool) to help you attain that purpose. When we team up, we both win. I'll inspire you to be your best and you'll work in great companies, moving them forward. You'll learn how to be in control of your money-making skills and use them to produce more and more value.

So, for the rest of this book, just think of you and me as a team, working together to build your company so we can build our economy!

WHY DO YOU NEED ME?

I'm a scientist. I love to observe, and over the last 30 years, I've been observing the relationships between bosses and employees.

I was raised by entrepreneurs, so our family's discussions around the dinner table always centered on the business (mostly its problems and frustrations). From an early age, I remember that our biggest issue was that we couldn't pay great people enough to keep them for long. As I grew up within that business and took on supervisory roles, I started to observe, and over time, I learned what makes a great employee and what makes an I-want-to-rip-my-hair-out-and-run-into-the-street-with-scissors employee. There was never a lot of extra cash to pay our employees more, so I felt that the best I could do for them was to provide an excellent training ground. However, I noticed this curious thing: when we found a rock star, someone who really produced amazing results—we *found* a way to pay them more!

When I was 24, I decided to leave the family businesses and get a *real* career. I was hired as the HR Manager for a large company that was in the middle of three mergers. I witnessed the meshing of cultures, the hiring of new employees, and the laying off of others. Always a scientist, I carefully observed when and why management teams decided to keep certain people and even gave them raises while others were laid off.

My next adventure took me into career counseling for professionals who wanted to get to the next level, mostly by changing jobs. I taught growth-seeking people how to define their next job *wants*, how to find jobs that didn't yet exist in the want ads, how to write a résumé, succeed in an interview, and negotiate the killer salary of their dreams! As I coached these dedicated people, I was able to get inside their heads and help them *see* their value, then *communicate* that value to potential employers. Additionally, I worked with companies that were downsizing to help the laid-off employees find new jobs. Again, as with my previous job, I was able to observe the type of people that they laid off and the type of people they kept. I've built those experiences into the tools in this book so you won't be caught on the wrong side.

A relocation had me on the move again and this time, because of my enduring love for coaching, I took a position in Educational Counseling, helping mid-career professionals make themselves more employable by gaining additional education. Again, I witnessed two different types of people who wanted to make better lives for themselves and their families. I noticed the differences between the people who were merely "checking the boxes" and those who really made an effort to understand and obtain marketable skills.

Fast forward ten years: I found myself as president of a CPA firm, which brought me back to my entrepreneurial roots. I thoroughly loved my role advising small businesses and 80% of the time, I was advising them about people issues. Their biggest asset was (and still is) their people. At the same time, their biggest headache and worry was (and still is) their *people*—keeping them happy, trained, paid, and productive. Once again, I was managing people myself and dealing with budgets, salaries, and productivity. It was while I was with the CPA firm that I fell in love with personal assessments. I love assessments because they add science to information that is otherwise subjective and open to interpretation. It was here that I found that I could learn 50% about a person just by looking at their assessments. (Check out the end of the book for a few of my favorites.) That brings us to today…if you're still reading this, thanks for sticking with me!

For the past six years, it's been my unique privilege to serve entrepreneurs as a business coach with my own business, TractionFirst, based in Dallas, Texas. As a business coach, I am welcomed into the inner circles of leadership teams of small, growth-oriented companies (10-250 employees). I know, at an intimate level, how these teams think, how they make their decisions, and even how they feel, and I get to coach them in their journeys to becoming their best. The system I use is EOS®, The Entrepreneurial Operating System, described in the book *Traction* by Gino Wickman. In this system, we use The Six Key Components™ to build a strong business:

VISION, PEOPLE, DATA, ISSUES, PROCESS, and TRACTION

Although it is important for all of these key components to be strong, I find that as we work through issues together, 80% of the issues lead back to the *people* component. Again, I've observed what bosses want and need out of their people (you!) as they literally create jobs in my session room each time we meet!

So, putting all of those experiences together, I created a toolbox for you.

The Earning Advantage Toolbox
will help bridge the gap between
what businesses need and what *you* want out of a career.

Let's get started!

SECTION 1
YOUR MINDSET

Whether you think you can or think you can't, you're right.

—Henry Ford

MYTHS YOU NEED TO STOP BELIEVING

Myth 1: Money can't buy happiness. (Bullcrap!)

Money used well can support our inner happiness, provide the resources for experiences, help us create and sustain important relationships, help us to help others, and help us gain access to additional knowledge.

Money is a tool to support happiness, if you are already happy.

Many clients I coached when they were searching for a new job had what I call "head trash" around the concept of money. They thought of it as bad or corrupt. If this is you, let it go. Money is a tool that can help you get what you want. It's not the goal, it helps you *meet* your goals. It's like gas in the car: more gas = more miles, more miles = more experiences, more experiences = more growth, more growth = more satisfaction.

Myth 2: The amount of money I can earn is determined by my position or my boss.

As capitalism started to flourish in the early days of the United States of America, people started to use the phrase, "making money."

Ayn Rand, the famous novelist and philosopher, pointed out that a long time ago, before the free market economy was an idea, money, wealth, and status were just passed down from generation to generation. She said, "No other language or nation had ever used these words [to make money] before; men had always thought of wealth as a static quantity—to be seized, begged, inherited, shared, looted or obtained as a favor. Americans were the first to understand that wealth has to be created." America provided immigrants with the right environment. Americans were free to work, free to fight, and free to be creative with the ways they lived and exchanged goods and services. Somewhere along the line, someone thought it was clever to announce that he was making money, and it stuck. The same is globally true today throughout the free nations. You get to *create* money for yourself. We still trade money for perceived value. Only always.

Myth 3: There is an easy way to make money.

There is not. Period.

THE BIG IDEA YOU NEED TO START BELIEVING

I'm a straight shooter. I'm not going to sugarcoat this for you: the only way to continuously make the money you want, to lead the happy life you want, is to *produce more measurable value.*

You need to produce more *and* show your boss that you have produced more.

One of America's favorite motivational icons, Zig Ziglar, is famous for saying,

> *"You will get what you want, if you help enough other people get what they want."*

STRATEGIES THAT DON'T WORK

If you are thinking about asking for a raise, please don't take advice from your friend's friend. If you've ever used one of the ineffective tactics I've listed below, don't fret. You can repent by using the Earning Advantage Toolbox. But there is a chance it will take you a bit longer if you've already sinned (*wink*)!

Let me tell it to you straight: my clients (remember, they are bosses) have seen and heard crazy tactics when employees ask for raises. Everything from: "Lunch is expensive downstairs; I need a raise so I can afford it," to "I'm saving up for a tattoo, so can I have a raise?"

In a survey of over 100 actual bosses, here is what they said they thought about the following tactics:

The employee used:	The boss was thinking:
Fear: "I'm going to leave if I don't get more money."	*Okay, leave.* *Not a team player.* *Not committed to his co-workers or the company.* *Not loyal.* *Short-sighted.*
Guilt: "I've been here for two years and have not received a raise."	*But you're still doing the same amount of work.* *So?* *What are you doing to better the company or yourself?*

Justification: "I do so much for this company; I should be making more."	*I feel bad I don't have more to offer her.* *We all should be making more.* *Does she know that I didn't pay myself last month to cover her paycheck?*
Shame: "My friend at _____ makes more than I do and works less hard."	*Then maybe you should work there too.* *I wonder if I'm a bad boss.* *How does the other company do it? What other corners are they cutting?* *That's a lie.*
Whining: "I need a raise because I have to pay for _____."	*We all have needs.* *Is it a need or a want?* *If he can't manage his money, can he manage his job?*

The main observation I made when I dug into these thoughts of bosses was that they were all *defensive*! If you use words like these when asking for a raise, your boss feels like they need to defend their position, or essentially, fight back. This is the worst position to be in when you are trying to get something you want. When any human feels defensive (think back to the caveman days), his or her brain releases a chemical that triggers protective reactions and the primitive part of the brain takes control. When talking to your boss about a raise, you want her to use the logical, evolved, and intelligent part of her brain—the one that can see and calculate the added value you bring.

Additionally, even if these strategies do work in the short term, notice how they set you up in the mind of your employer as weak and not the kind of employee that can produce for the company long-term.

The tools I'm going to teach you will set you up for a lifetime of continual increases in your money-making!

You'll continue to make more money because you'll consistently produce value wherever you are.

WHAT DO I MEAN BY "PRODUCING VALUE?"

To understand this, let's have a quick look at how money flows through a business.

The QDV (Quick and Dirty Version): Let's say the business you work for sold $10 million worth of product in a year. After factoring in the expenses of running the business and buying all of the material needed to make the product, most companies are considered healthy if they have 10% profit—some more, some less—but we'll stick with an average of 10% because the math is easy for me! (I don't do math in public... but wait, this book is pretty public, wouldn't you say?)

What happens to all that money???

$10,000,000	Income: Cash from sales of the product
-$9,000,000	Expenses: Cost of the materials, equipment, and labor it takes to run the business
=$1,000,000	Profit! The owner's money, right? (Wrong)

So, the profit is $1 million. That goes in the owner's pocket, right? Wrong! Most people think that the word profit means that the owner is dancing in the dollars.

That $1,000,000 is now taxed, usually at a rate around 50%, so now we are down to $500,000. If you are running a $10 million business, the amount of your next month's expenses is probably about $300,000, so you need to keep *at least* that amount in the bank account to pay your bills the following month. Makes sense, right?

$1,000,000	Profit—yeah!
-$500,000	Taxes (sadly)
-$300,000	Needed to pay next month's bills
=$200,000	This amount needs to cover emergencies, additional equipment, new growth plans, etc.

Now we are down to $200,000. That is the amount available to cover emergencies, purchase additional equipment, add or upgrade technology or vehicles, or build and maintain additional locations in order to grow the business. It is not nearly enough to stay ahead of the game, so some owners choose to take on debt or seek investors so they can continue to grow the business, which opens up an entire new expense: interest.

You don't need any more detail than that but here's the big idea:

The owner needs you!

If you can help the business either increase income or decrease expenses, you will produce more value for the business.

If you were able to increase the sales by $50,000 or reduce the expenses by $50,000, you've produced additional value. That's what every company is trying to do: increase sales, decrease costs. If you wrap your head around that, you'll know what it means to produce value. Most business owners *want* to pay you more when you produce more.

Consider Greg's story:

He never asked; he just produced great results. Changes were afoot. Some people in the company were just there for a paycheck and consistently producing results well below the target, but Greg's results were above the target. The owners of the firm were consistently able to bill 80% of his hours worked when the target was 65%. Being a salaried employee, Greg consistently produced more value for the company than they paid him for. When his manager looked at the history, this had been happening for eight months! The manager gave Greg a raise he didn't ask for and everyone was happy.

Sounds like a great story, right? After you learn the Earning Advantage way, come back to this story and think about what Greg could have done to make this happen sooner.

PRODUCING MEANINGFUL WORK

Somebody somewhere will want me to mention that money isn't everything, and they're right. Many employee engagement studies show that experiencing meaningful work is at least as important as a paycheck. In his book *Start with Why*, Simon Sinek (one of my favorites) explains that it's not what we do or how we do it that's important, it's *why* we do it. So…what is your *why*? Why do you go to work every day? Remember, money is the tool; why do you need or want that tool? (Do an Internet search for "Simon Sinek Start with Why," then watch the 18-minute TED Talk for inspiration.)

My Why:

_____

_____

_____

Aha moment: Your why makes your work meaningful to you.

When I see the words *meaningful work*, I immediately think *productivity*. No matter what *meaningful* means to you, it indicates that you are producing value for someone else. As an exercise, see if you can think of what the following jobs produce as *meaningful work*. Think big and think deep. What are they producing? I've done the first few for you.

- Trash collector: a clean city
- A roofer: a warm, dry house
- Cashier at a movie theatre _____
- Shelf stocker at a grocery store _____
- Assembly line worker in a steel factory _____
- Cable TV installer _____
- Swimming pool salesperson _____
- A marketing assistant _____
- An accountant _____
- Your position _____

WILL YOU BE A PRODUCER?

There are two types of people (and we are all both of these types during different parts of our day). Today, I worked with a team for nine hours in a long, tough session, and *produced* results for them. Now, I'm sitting on a plane headed back to Texas *consuming* the services of Southwest Airlines (I love them, by the way). The key to becoming and claiming that you are a producer is to be conscious of it. Commit to being more of a producer than a consumer. This mindset applies not just within the economy; it works with energy, too.

Do you know anyone at work who consistently produces energy?

When they are around, people just get more done. These people have a way of activating others to move. Maybe they make the day go by faster by adding laughter or maybe their presence makes the workplace a little happier. Maybe it's just their personal work ethic that is a good example for others.

How about the opposite: *Do you know someone at work who consumes energy?*

They sap the energy of those around them and things get done a little slower! Often times, they can be found gossiping, complaining, coming to work late or not at all…you get me?

Commit to being aware of when you are producing and when you are consuming for the next week. Then, think about how it feels to be a producer, to be the one that's driving to *get it done* for the rest of the team. It feels awesome 100% of the time!

Do this quick exercise to get you thinking about how to perform like a producer.

I'm a Producer when I...	I'm a Consumer when I...
How does it feel? _____	How does it feel? _____

Producers like to surround themselves with (hire) other producers (of results and energy). Read what some of my clients have said about this:

"I'll pay someone a thousand dollars a day if they can sell $5,000 a day!"

"You can work as many hours as you want. I have an endless list of projects I need done that I can't get around to."

"I'd love to pay my hard-working employees more, in fact, one of our company's long term goals is for our employees to be the highest paid in the industry. We'll only get there if everyone is producing."

"One guy in our office has a contagious laugh. It seems like everyone just gets more done when he's around."

Big Idea: People who are producers of results and energy will get paid more.

And now...let's get into the head of your boss.

SECTION 2
YOUR BOSS'S MINDSET

The best leaders are humble enough to realize
their victories depend on their people.
—John C. Maxwell

How do I know what's in your bosses' heads? They let me in!
Read on to hear some thoughts that they usually don't (or
won't) say.

YOUR BOSS IS THINKING, *I WANT TO PROMOTE YOU.*

I've spent over 5,000 hours with leadership teams, reviewing previous quarters and planning for future quarters. An important question that often comes up is: Do we need more people? When the answer is yes, (rarely is it no), we literally *create* jobs. We decide what we need this new person to be accountable for, then go on a search to find this person. 95% of the time the team would rather promote someone at the company into these newly created roles than hire a new employee. Your boss *wants you* to fill these new positions. Here's why:

- It's a new position, but *you* already know how to work in the company. They don't need to worry that you won't fit in, show up, or work hard to produce results because you already do!

- *You* can train someone who already exists within the company to fill your old position. Your present position is known to the company and probably has documented processes attached to it. It's much easier to hire a new person for an old job than it is to hire a new person for a new job.

Then why don't they just promote me?

Here's the issue: when we create these jobs, the first thing I ask the leadership team is, "Is there someone in the company who could fill this role now?" Disappointingly, the answer is often no. The tools I teach you in the next section will help you become the person that makes the leadership team say *yes*! So, keep in mind that if given the choice, your boss would rather promote *you* to the new position!

YOUR BOSS IS THINKING, *PLEASE, MAKE MY LIFE EASIER.*

The best days for your manager are the days when you step up. If you can focus on making their life easier, they'll look to you for more and more responsibility. Taking on more responsibility leads to more productivity and is the best way to earn more money for the long term. Here is a list of some common ways that you can make your manager's life easier:

Show up: Absenteeism is a chronic problem across all industries and causes a flash of terror in the eyes of a boss when someone calls in sick or worse, doesn't call at all. No matter how good you are or how pleasant you are to work with, you'll never make the money you desire if your boss can't count on you to simply show up.

Consider this rule: the only reason to not be at work is vacation or death (your death). It's a little bold, but you get my point. If you don't feel good, there's a medication for that. Get yourself together and (provided you're not contagious) get to work!

Get it done on time: Bosses want to see more "get 'er done" and getting it done on time. They long for more enthusiasm, energy, and focus in getting the project completed for the customer. If you can increase your dedication to on-time job completion by just 10%, it will be noticed.

Smile: It goes a long way!

Be positive about the possibilities: I think I can have this done a day early if I don't get distracted.

Verbally encourage someone else: *We can do this, guys!*

Come to work 10 minutes early, and get to work: Not just for the coffee.

Stay 10 minutes late: Even if it's to breathe, reflect, and plan the next day.

Make customers say "wow": Tie the bow. One of the companies I coach has a "we tie the bow" approach to customer service. Instead of getting the customer only what they need, they make it look good and do more than they said they would. Could you do this for your customers?

Solve your problems: Think it through before you run to the boss for every little thing. Use the resources available before you go to the boss (manuals, documented processes, coworkers, Google it). This shows that you are resourceful and that you engage in thinking instead of just doing.

YOUR BOSS IS THINKING,
I'D RATHER LEAD THAN MANAGE.

Maybe you already know this, but there are differences between management and leadership, and here is the biggest one: for most of the bosses I work with, leadership is fun and rewarding. On the other hand, management is uncomfortable, repetitive, and boring. To help illustrate the point, here is a list of some of the differences between leadership and management as described in the book *How to Be a Great Boss* by Gino Wickman and René Boer:

Leadership	Management
• Working *on* the future of the business	• Working *in* the business
• Inspiring direction	• Setting expectations and tracking goals
• Creating opportunities for growth	• Communicating positive and negative feedback
• Thinking	• Making sure the *doing* gets done

YOUR BOSS IS THINKING,
WHAT WILL YOUR
CONTRIBUTION BE?

Bosses divide employees into four types. Your boss might have different names or may not even be conscious of the types, but the concept still applies. To describe the four types, we use two categories: Core Values and Performance.[1]

Spoiler Alert: To be a producer (your ultimate goal), you need to be strong in the Core Values *and* the Performance categories.

The Core Values of a company describe how a person should act within the company. If your company has Core Values and lives them, you probably can rattle them off, your boss often asks you how you feel about the Core Values, and they regularly recognize people in the company for demonstrating the valued behaviors. If you don't have Core Values at your company, reflect on these concepts: *I'm pleasant to work with* or *I am helpful, cooperative, and have a good attitude at work.*

Performance is simply how well you do your job. Do you get your job done well and on time?

---

[1] This concept is adapted from the "Values Performance Matrix" designed by Jack Welch, a former GE executive.

Now we have the set-up for the descriptions of the four different types of employees.

The Star

First, we have the star. The star is the preferred type of employee. Stars are pleasant to work with, they are a joy to have around, and they help other people. They also do good work! They make few mistakes and when they do, they learn from them. Stars pay attention to quality and efficiency. They are star employees! Newsflash: The stars make the money, and the stars are the examples for the rest of the company. If you're not a star already, your best bet at making money within the company is to work your way into this category. The work we'll do in this book will help you get there.

Exercise: Think of someone in the company who is a star. (Keep this person in mind; you may want to observe their behavior or get some tips from them in the near future.)

A star _____

It takes a while to become a star. When I was 17, I had my first supervisory position, and it didn't take me long to figure out that if I just hired the right kind of person (easy to get along with, positive, generally happy), I could teach them the skills they needed to do the job. In this grid, this type of person is called a puppy.

The Puppy

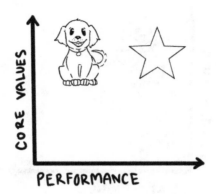

Puppies share the Core Values of the company. They are eager and willing and excited, but they must be trained in order to be productive. Puppies are on their way to being stars and have the highest potential, but it takes some time and a boss who is willing to invest in them. Growing companies love to hire puppies, but they realize it costs time and money to turn them into stars. If you're a puppy, you'll want to work your way toward becoming a star by becoming more productive. Then, you'll have the best chance of making the most money.

Exercise: Think of someone who is a puppy (either at your current job or in the past).

The Puppies _____

What do they need, in your opinion, to make it to the star category? (This is just to increase your observation skills, so feel free to brainstorm. There are no wrong answers.)

_____

_____

_____

The Rats (star spelled backwards!)

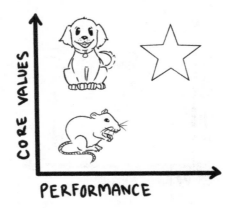

Rats are employees that are *in hiding*. They are probably just pleasant enough to not get fired and produce just enough to not get fired. My clients (the bosses) will give them a chance to change their ways. Usually rats scurry; they don't like to put effort into their lives (so sad), and they hop from job to job, trying to hide in the corners. They live their lives in a dreary grey. Rats never make the real money. It takes a lot of effort for a rat to change, but I've seen it happen. If this is you, you've got some work to do.

Exercise: Think of a rat in your company (or in a past company). Sometimes they are the bullies; they don't want others to produce because it will shine a light of accountability on them.

The rats _____

What is it that you can specifically point to that puts them in this category?

_____

_____

_____

The Terrorist

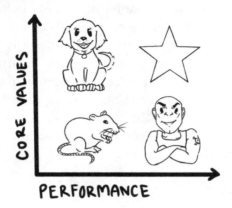

These employees are called terrorists because it's as though they have a bomb strapped to their chest when they say to the boss, "I double dare you to fire me; you can't! I am too productive; you'd never make it without me!" Essentially, they hold the company hostage with their bad attitudes. Terrorists often are loved by the customers but loathed inside the company. Because they are high producers, they think they don't need to be team players or follow company procedures. Terrorists might also be observed holding information close to themselves, fearing that if it was released, their skills would no longer be needed. They very rarely will offer to share their know-how with others. I've also heard them called *toxic geniuses*.

I've only witnessed a terrorist reform twice. In both circumstances, it was long and grueling and took a lot of cooperation from both the boss and the terrorist. Healthy companies are wise and get rid of terrorists.

If you are holding your company hostage, stop it! Although you are *producing* results, you are *consuming* energy from the other parts of the company. The sum total is that in the long run, you are not producing the total effect that will move the company forward. You won't last long, especially with growth-oriented companies that realize culture builds a better bottom line. If you are reading this and have just been shocked into realizing that this is you, there is good news: the skills in this book are your best bet for reform. Read on!

Exercise: Think of a terrorist in your company or in a past company. Need another hint? Sometimes, their boss tries to shelter them, treats them differently, or does not make them follow the same rules as everyone else because the boss is being terrorized. Anyone come to mind?

The terrorist _____

List the ways in which they are holding the company back.

_____

_____

_____

The big idea: Bosses appreciate a great attitude, but attitude alone won't get you \$\$\$. You need both a great attitude (shared Core Values) and great performance! The two added together produce present and future productivity!

Self-Assessment

It's time for the moment of truth. Get some Oreos and put on your big boy pants! It's time to get real. There are so many people in this world who want a job but not as many who really want to work!

> **Let's take a deep breath together and
> do a checkup from the neck up!
> So, how's your mindset?**

I can't do the believing for you, except to say that the world needs you to step up. Will you?

Circle the number that best corresponds to your ranking in the following:

I believe I'm in charge of my earning ability.

1 2 3 4 5 6 7 8 9 10

I am *excited* about being more of a producer than a consumer.

1 2 3 4 5 6 7 8 9 10

I know that producing more value is the only way to consistently make the money I want.

1 2 3 4 5 6 7 8 9 10

Where are you in the Core Values/Performance grid?

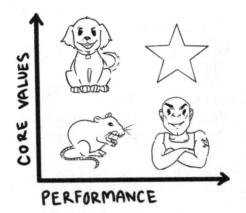

How do you rank in accordance with your company's Core Values and Performance requirements?

Are you a puppy wanting more training? Are you a star wanting more autonomy or responsibility? Or ugh…are you a rat that needs to step it up in your performance, habits, and attitude? (Do it!) And dare I ask: are you a terrorist holding the company and those around you hostage? Rate yourself and identify the next step to get you into the star category.

I am a _____.

I need to _____ as my next step in becoming a star.

How are your habits?

There are many books on great work habits and productivity tools, but I boil it down to these basics. Essentially, if you don't have these, bosses don't even want to talk about your earning potential.

Basic good habits	How are you doing?
Be on time: This is so simple and really a no-brainer, but it's a chronic problem. When you don't show up on time, the perception people have of you is that you are not organized, not enthusiastic about the job, not loyal, and not interested in moving yourself forward.	I am on time to work. Yes or No
Work on purpose: Stay on task and within the scope of what needs to be done. Focus—don't get distracted. Know the priorities of the job/department and know what success looks like.	I keep my focus on the priorities of the job. Yes or No
Show up: Rarely, if at all, take an unscheduled day off.	I rarely take an unscheduled day off (once per year). Yes or No
Positivity: Have a we-can-do-it attitude, then be an asset in figuring out how to solve problems.	I am positive at work. Yes or No
Say please and thank you: Yes, Mom was right, this *does* matter.	I say "please" and "thank you." Yes or No

Appearance: When your image improves, your performance improves. Make it a point to come to work dressed just a little better than needed. If you need to wear the uniform, make sure it looks great. If you wear a T-shirt with a logo, tuck it in. If jeans are acceptable, make sure they are clean and in good condition.	I look better than I need to at work. Yes or No
Be a team player: In his book *The Ideal Team Player*, Patrick Lencioni maintains that three adjectives that describe a team player are: Humble (Give others credit, abhor arrogance.) Hungry (for results...Yay! Productivity!) Smart (*people smart*: know how to handle and work with people.)	I am a team player. Yes or No

If you have issues with any of the above...
Here is a quick way to solve them all:

DO IT!

You don't need months of therapy or re-training, you just need to *decide* that today is a new day and that you now follow these habits.

Motivational expert Tom Ziglar says: "The fastest way to success is to replace bad habits with good habits." Start small if you need to, but the faster you create great habits, the faster you'll get what you want!

Start practicing these habits today and see how many people notice; I bet your boss will notice by day three!

Let's do a quick recap of what we've learned and what we've agreed to.

You've learned about some new mindsets!

- Money can buy happiness, if you are already happy!

- The only way to consistently make more money is to produce more value!

- Great work habits are the foundation of increased pay.

- Bosses pay more for stars in the company.

- *You* are in control of what you earn.

Now you're ready...So roll up your sleeves and get to work on learning and implementing the tools that will get you producing value!

SECTION 3
YOUR TOOLBOX

You were born to win, but to be the winner you were born to be, you have to plan to win and prepare to win. Then and only then can you expect to win.

—Zig Ziglar

Imagine that it's your first day on the job. You arrive early and someone is there to greet you. They direct you to where you'll be working for the day, show you the project, and leave. You want to make a good first impression, so you look around to see what you have to work with.

You're looking for tools. Tools help us be more productive. Can you imagine designing a graphic, installing carpet, laying concrete, balancing a bank account, cleaning an office, or writing a professional document without any tools? Never! Humans separate themselves from the rest of the animal kingdom because we invent and use tools!

Every great producer needs a toolbox to carry their tools. I've put together a toolbox to help you build your productivity machine. The toolbox will help you visualize and organize these methods in your mind. Within the toolbox are four compartments that will hold your tools and keep them organized. There are a total of eight tools. Here's a picture of what your toolbox will look like when it's complete:

The See It Compartment will help you see things in your company in a new way.
Tools:
Big Picture Boot Camp
Weekly Numbers Microscope

The Say It Compartment will teach you the words to use that will help you make more money.
Tools:
Same Team
TALK

The Solve It Compartment will help you focus on solving issues in your department so you can show that you know how to produce.
Tools:
Where's my Puzzle Piece?
Issues Solving Track™

The Serve Compartment will help you use all of the other sections together to ensure that you become an influence for productivity in your company, securing your money-making potential forever.
Tools:
A Go-To Person
Use the Coach Approach

COMPARTMENT 1

SEE IT

Helping you see your company in a new light

Your first step in this journey will be to simply observe. Observe the workings of the company as if you were learning about how a machine works. You'll want to inspect all of the elements that need to be in place for the machine to produce. It might be very obvious what the big, noisy parts do, but what about that hose in the back—what does it do? Why is it there? What would happen if you clamped it off? You will have lots of questions, some assumptions, and some *aha* moments as you observe the machine doing its thing. You need to do the same with the company you work for.

Jill's note: Not all things you observe will be pretty or tied with a beautiful bow. No company is perfect, nor should it be. Success is a poor teacher and when companies are imperfect, there is fertile ground for innovation. In fact, if you start looking at the company and see more broken parts than you thought you'd find, pat yourself on the back—this company is in need of your help (and that's productive work, my friend). But I'm getting ahead of myself...

It's time to learn how to use our first tool in the See It Compartment.

Tool: Big Picture Boot Camp

Have you ever been to a boot camp? Boot camps are designed to kickstart you into producing. For most of us, when we hear the words *boot camp*, we think of the military or an intense physical workout. Most boot camps have a couple of things in common:

1. They throw you in without a lot of warm up.

2. They push you out of your comfort zone.

3. The training you do builds in intensity as you go.

This tool will do all of the above.

In order to accelerate your observation of the company, I've created this tool to help you make the best observations, quickly. It's also designed to kickstart your brain into thinking strategically.

> Thinking is the hardest work there is, which
> is probably the reason so few engage in it.
> —Henry Ford

Not everyone has the natural talent for strategic, future-focused thinking, but that's why we have tools. Tools accelerate our productivity, right? This tool will accelerate your strategic thinking. Just like we go to a gym to work our muscles, this tool will build your thinking muscle. By turning on more of your thinking skills, you'll become more valuable to your company.

Preparation: Schedule a two-hour block of time in a place where you can be alone, undisturbed, and free of distractions. (Put your phone away, too.)

Materials: This book, or the downloadable workbook (or a separate notebook), and a pencil.

What to do: Think about, then write the answers to the questions on the next page.

Jill's tips:

- Just like working out with a personal trainer, these questions will get harder as we go.

- At this point, there are no wrong answers. If you don't know, guess. Guessing is coming up with the best answer using only the data you have access to. (It's not a wild guess.)

- Spend just as much time (or more) thinking about the answers. Remember, the goal is to get you to think, not to write.

- Your writing is just for you; don't be worried about spelling, complete sentences, or get hung up on word choice. If you understand it, it's good enough.

- Simplicity is your friend. What is the simplest answer? Simplicity is the work of geniuses; any idiot can create something complex.

- Take a break about every 30-45 minutes—just a short one to drink something, breathe, and move your body. Don't pick up that phone, though. Stay focused, just move your body. That will help your brain work better.

Okay, that was your warm-up. Now, go.

Big Picture Boot Camp Questions

1. What does my company sell?

_____

_____

2. Why do people buy what my company sells?

_____

_____

3. Why does my company matter to the world?

_____

_____

4. How do we sell our product/service?

_____

_____

5. How do we deliver our product/service?

_____

_____

6. What do we promise our customers? (Hint: Check the website, but don't get distracted.)

_____

_____

7. What are the types of costs involved in selling that product/service?

_____

_____

8. What are the costs of producing our product/service?

_____

_____

9. What problems arise when mistakes are made?

_____

_____

10. What problem does our product/service solve?

_____

_____

11. What need does my department fill?

_____

_____

12. What does my boss worry about?

_____

_____

13. What problem is my boss trying to solve?

_____

_____

14. What is my boss trying to understand?

_____

_____

15. What does the *best* employee in my department do differently than the rest?

_____

_____

16. How do I know that I've done a good job today?

_____

_____

YOU DID IT!

Congratulations on finishing the Big Picture Boot Camp!

Note: If you didn't finish in two hours, schedule as many two-hour blocks of time with yourself until you feel you've answered all the questions. In between your boot camp sessions, do additional research on industry websites and your company website. Interview stars in your company, etc., until you feel you have a good idea of what the big picture looks like.

Bonus exercise (for those who like to work ahead): Go back through your answers and underline areas that require more information. This will be important when you get to the Say It Compartment of your toolbox.

Double Bonus (for the super over-achievers): Go back through your notes again and circle the areas where you think you could contribute solutions or improvements. This will be handy when we get to the Solve It Compartment of the toolbox.

Tool: Weekly Numbers Microscope

Now that you've observed the big picture, let's get granular by studying the numbers that are important to your boss, your department, and your company. Measuring is very compelling for humans. We love to measure things because often, statistics define success.

In the same way you probably measure your gas mileage or your weight loss (or sometimes gain, gulp!), I want you to start measuring things at work. The work you produce needs to be measured. Measuring productivity with numbers is the *best* way to show increased results. It's how you know you are winning.

If your company currently measures using objective, clear data, this will be easier for you. If not, you'll need to start measuring some things on your own. Weekly numbers are better to track than monthly numbers. If a weekly number is lower than your goal, you have 52 chances in the year to make adjustments. When you measure things on a monthly basis, you only have 12 chances to make changes. So, when you are looking for numbers, think in terms of weekly measurements.

Typical Company Measurables by Department

Marketing	Sales	Operations	Finance	Administration
Number of clicks on the website	Number of calls made	Amount of waste	Accounts Receivable over 60 days	Number of incoming phone calls
Leads that called in	Number of face-to-face appointments	Overtime hours worked	Cash on hand	Number of job openings
Where the lead came from	Number of webinars scheduled with prospects	Customer complaints	Credit available	Number of interviews scheduled
Amount of leads added to database	Number of proposals sent	Utilization rates of equipment	Number of clients denied credit	Amount of IT tickets opened or closed
Qualified leads ratio	$$ in the pipeline	Utilization rates of labor force	Overdue payables	Employee satisfaction rate
Meetings with centers of influence	Sales booked	Machine downtime for repairs	Warranty claims	Employee sick days
Newsletter responses	Number of cancellations after free trial period	Billable hours worked	Input errors	Travel expenses

Preparation:

1. Look around the company for numbers that are already measured, and make a list of them. Maybe your boss always publishes the amount of sales made each day on a board. Maybe your supervisor tells the department how much waste accumulated for each run of a machine. Maybe there is a sign posting how many days the company has had without an accident, etc.

   What my company already measures and reports to me:

   _____

   _____

   _____

2. Schedule a two-hour block of time to implement the Weekly Numbers Microscope Tool (distraction-free again).

   What to do: Using the grid above and your observations to help you think about and write down the answers to these questions.

   Which numbers are important to your department? (List all of them that you can think of.)

   _____

   _____

   _____

   Now, what three numbers does your boss count on *you* to deliver?

   _____

   _____

   _____

Now, let's use the tools together to refine our machine. Think about and write the answers to the questions below.

What is my role in the company *now*? Now that you see more of the big picture, and you've identified the numbers that are important to your position, what role do you play? Use your observations from the Big Picture Boot Camp and the Weekly Numbers Microscope to write a bit about your part in the company right now.

Now, think about your future in the company (start with three to six months from now). It is most likely that the business you are working in wants to grow. If it does not want to grow, it is at risk for extinction.

The companies I love to work with have a "grow or die" mentality. The day they think they are done growing is they day they start dying. And it's the same with you. So, how do you see your role in the future? What do you think the department needs in the future? Predict what your boss will say when you ask the questions, "What is my role in the future of the company? How can I help this company/department grow? What additional tasks can I take on?"

You'll ask these questions for real in a bit, but for now, answer them using what you learned while using the Big Picture Boot Camp and the Weekly Numbers Microscope tools.

Okay, I'll be quiet. Write your thoughts…I'll wait!

If you are struggling with this, that's normal! Don't feel you need to have all the answers. In the next section, you'll learn how to ask great questions to fill in your answers.

So, with that, on to the next compartment of your toolbox!

SAY IT

Communicating with your boss: Using the right words to increase your productivity

During my time as a career coach, I met with a frustrated salesperson who had been passed over for a promotion. I asked him if his boss knew that he wanted the position. He looked at me puzzled and said, "Of course, he knew." Upon digging further, the only thing he'd really verbalized to his boss was, "Hey, you know you can count on me, right?" Those were the exact words that he used to tell his boss that he wanted the job! When communicating with your boss about the value you produce and the money you'll be earning, you'll need to be very specific and also be willing to say it more than once! With the tools in this compartment, you'll learn that we shouldn't beat around the bush or assume that anyone knows anything. You know what they say about assuming—*it makes an "ass" out of "u" and "me"!*

Myth: Don't say things to your boss that they don't want to hear.

FACT: Business owners and bosses want and need you to speak the direct truth.

Tool: Same Team

Have you ever watched young children play soccer? It's the funniest thing—no matter what their jersey color is, they all run for the ball. I once attended a game where the coach's biggest challenge was to get the players to play as a team. Everyone wanted to kick the ball, and they would often kick the ball out from under their own teammate. The coach would scream from the sidelines, "Same team. Same team!" Playing like this makes no sense. But often, that's exactly how employees feel, like they are on a different team than their boss. This tool will help you be on the same team as your boss.

To get on the same team as your boss, you start by being *open* and *honest*.

Dedicate yourself to being *open:*

Open means that you are open to possibilities. You are open to new solutions. You are open to others' ideas for improvement. The opposite of open (closed) is thinking that there is no way to fix something. Closed thoughts or conversations sound like this: "That would never work." Or, "We don't have time for that." Or, "We've always done it that way." Closed language puts you on the opposite team.

Here are a few phrases that help you sound *open*:

"Hmmm, I've never thought of it that way."
"That might work."
"I'd like to hear what you think about that."
"What else might be contributing to this problem?"

Now, write a few phrases of your own that sound open:

_____

_____

_____

Dedicate yourself to being *honest*:

Honest, in this tool, means that you just say it. If there is something that needs to be said, just say it. You don't need to butter people up or get a lot of people on your side before you have honest conversations. Just get the issue on the table. Being honest does not involve being mean or gossiping. Honesty means that you bring the issues *to the people who can solve them*. The opposite of honesty is grumbling or complaining to your family or coworkers but never bringing the issue to your boss.

Here are a few phrases that are honest:

"I've noticed that several people in the department don't know how to use the order entry program. Is there something I could do to help them learn it?"
"Yesterday on the job, we threw away scraps that I think could have been used on other jobs. Is that something we should work on in the future?"
"It took me three hours to complete the invoicing today and it normally takes only

one. The computer seemed slow. Is there something I can do to speed it up?"

Notice that the comment is right to the point, but it is also paired with an offer to help.

Open + Honest + Offer = Happy Boss

Write some of your own honest + offer statements:

_____

_____

_____

If you are the one that brings up issues or solutions with an attitude of "I'm here to help," you'll be seen as a producer, someone who really cares about getting this company to the next level. It will be noticed, appreciated, and *valued*. Using these statements will soon have you on the same team as your boss.

Tool: The TALK

What is the right way to talk to your boss about making more money? In my research and coaching with bosses, there is a right and wrong way to do this. The TALK tool stands for *Timing*, *Attitude*, *Language*, and *Keep it going*.

T: Timing

Schedule a time to talk with your boss; don't drop this on them in the middle of the lunch room. The best time to schedule this is when feelings are calm and clear. If the plant is pushing out a tricky shipment that week, or if someone has just quit—that's a *bad* time to have this conversation. It will be more difficult for you and your boss to have these proactive discussions during chaotic times. This first conversation should be about 30 minutes long and should start and end on time. Even if you are having a great conversation, be respectful of your boss's time, and with five minutes left in the meeting, start to wrap it up with the Wrap-Up Question below.

A: Attitude

Approach this with a humble, happy, and positive attitude. Know that this is a journey. This does not need to be (nor will it be) perfect.

L: Language

If your boss gave you this book and said, "Let's talk in a few weeks," follow this TALK pattern. If your boss has no idea what you are up to, read below for your specific *L* in the TALK pattern (it's a bit different than the one here).

Thank You Statement: "Thanks for taking the time to talk with me today."

Opening Question: "I've done the work in that book you gave me, and I'm hoping you can fill in some answers that I couldn't find on my own."

Meaty Questions: Using the Big Picture Boot Camp and the Weekly Numbers Microscope exercises, have a conversation about your questions and answers. Choose two or three topics that really interest you or two or three topics that gave you the biggest *aha* during the exercises. There is no need to discuss all of them.

Wrap-up Question: End the conversation with: "I'm excited about producing more value for the company and for you, as my boss. What would you suggest is the best use of my time so that I start on the path of earning more money?" Listen, take notes, and make a plan with your boss as to the next step.

A note about taking notes: Take notes during your conversation. You are likely to be a bit nervous and might forget some details, so it will be nice to have notes.

Follow-up Question: "Thanks again for taking time to talk to me about this. When can we talk again?" My suggestion is two-four weeks, but get your boss's suggestion, too.

Follow-up Action Plan: Within 24 hours, write down the plan you and your boss agreed to (keep it simple, use bullet points) and send it to him/her as well. This is not so that you can hold your boss to what he/she said or some kind of legal CYA (cover your ass) tactic. I want you to write it down and send it to your boss for two major reasons.

- First: It is scientifically proven that when you write something down, you are more likely to do it. This is *your* commitment to the plan, not his or hers.

- Second: Communication! When your boss reads your account of the conversation, they will be able to clear up any misunderstandings right from the beginning. As a byproduct, they'll also think highly of your follow-up and communication skills.

Note: See Appendix B at the end of this book for a template of a simple action plan.

K: Keep it going

This first conversation is just the starting point on your path to making more money, so...

Make sure you have the second conversation!

This is so crucial! Talk about the Big Picture Boot Camp and Weekly Numbers Microscope Tools, and be excited to show where you've added productivity over the last four weeks. You can also add in some results from the Solve It Compartment. Ask for feedback from your boss using this question during the second (and next) TALK conversations:

"Is this path I'm on adding value to you, the department, and the company?"
If the answer is yes, keep going.
If it's no, ask "What *can* I do to be more productive?"

This shows that you are willing to produce added value before you expect additional money. This also sets you up as a person who is in it to win it for the long term, not a short-term-thinking person who wants instant gratification.

This is great, but when do I ask for the raise?

When you've been able to show added productivity (this means the numbers prove it), open up the money conversation again. Here are some sentences to get comfortable with:

"Thank you for helping me see the importance of reducing waste in the shop. Because of the plan we created, the shop now saves $1,000 per month in supplies. I'm excited to start on the next project and would like to also talk about an increased hourly rate? Is now a good time?"

Write your own money question:
Thank you for: _____

_____

_____

Because of (the action): _____

_____

_____

The company now (the results): _____

_____

_____

I'm excited to start the next project *and* would like to talk about an increased hourly rate/ salary/ commission. Is now a good time?

Most likely, your boss will ask you what kind of increase you have in mind. Consider this story when you are thinking of your answer:

> *During an all-company meeting of an indoor amusement venue, some of the employees were complaining about their hourly pay rate. After heated public discussions, one of the supervisors spoke up, saying to the disgruntled staff, "When I interviewed you, I asked what you wanted to be paid. Most of you asked for $8, some $9, but I was authorized to pay up to $12. Not one of you asked for $12."*

Ask for what you want. If you don't ask, you'll never get it.

The TALK: Take Two

If you bought this book on your own and your boss has no idea what you are up to, the conversation will be a bit different.

We still follow the TALK pattern, but with a few twists.
Step 1: Read the entire TALK Tool above.
Step 2: Replace the L (Language) with these words.

Take some time to prepare your questions and practice them. Write them down, and take them with you to the meeting. The conversation outline below is a suggestion. These questions might seem bold, and each word has a specific psychological reason for being there, so I highly suggest you memorize them, if possible!

Thank You Statement: Thanks for taking time to talk with me today.

Opening Question: I've been doing some thinking, and I'd really like to do more for you, the department, and the company so that I could *eventually* earn more money. Would you be willing to help me figure out ways I could do that?

Meaty Questions (choose a few): How can I best help the department? (Take notes.)
What else? (Take notes.)
How about _____? (Include your suggestions from the Solve It and Big Picture Boot Camp sections.)
What is the best use of my time? What else? How about _____?
What do you wish I knew how to do?
Is there someone that I could mentor/train for you?
What should I be reading/researching so I can be of more use to you?
How can I make your job easier?

Wrap-up Question: What is the best next step for me to be more valuable to you?

Follow-up Question: Thank you for your time today. Can we talk again in a few weeks? (Two-four weeks.)

Be prepared: If your boss did not hand you this book, it is likely that this will take you more time. Be patient, and keep using the tools. Your boss is most likely not used to this behavior from employees. It might take your boss a while to realize that you are on his or her team. Just like any other team, it will take a while for you all to get in step with each other.

Time to write your script!

Thank You Statement:

_____

_____

Opening Question:

_____

_____

Meaty Question(s):

_____

_____

Wrap-Up Question:

_____

_____

Follow-Up Question:

_____

_____

When you leave this conversation, remember to follow up with your written plan. Some of that plan should be the solutions you'll start working on. Now, on to Solve It.

SOLVE IT

Where you'll learn to solve problems that add to the productivity of your role

This is where you'll be able to make a productive contribution right away. Being able to solve problems within your position, department, or company will prove to your boss that you can be productive now *and* in the future.

When solving a problem, first you need to observe and identify where the problems are. This is what we did in the Big Picture Boot Camp. If you have not already done so, go back to your notes, and look for things that need fixing.

List them here:

_____

_____

Jill's note: If something seems obvious to you, but no one else is addressing it, it may be that *you* are the only one seeing it! When I work with leadership teams to solve issues, sometimes all the information they need is with the front-line employees. You do the work every day; you are the expert on how to solve front line issues.

Tool: Where's My Puzzle Piece?

Now we are going to narrow your focus! You can see the Big Picture, and you are starting to understand the part you play. Think of yourself as one piece of a larger puzzle. In your current position, you have a unique contribution to make. You can make the finished picture clearer. You have an impact to make, but if you try to do too many things at once or start recommending changes you can't implement, you won't make much headway. With the Puzzle Piece Tool, I'll teach you how to focus on one of those issues you uncovered in the See It and Say It Compartments.

How to use the Puzzle Piece Tool:

First, locate your department on the left-hand side of the table. Your company may call it something different than I have, so here are some quick definitions to see where you fit best. If you are working in a company where everyone does everything, choose a *department* that you are most excited about or where you are currently working the most (and see Appendix A!).

Marketing is communicating with the outside world about who we are and what we do. The goal of marketing is to know what our customers want and to bring in leads of potential new customers.

Sales is taking those leads and turning them into customers. Getting a potential customer to say, "Yes, I want to do business with your company!"

Operations is making the product or delivering the service. Essentially, following through on the promises that marketing and sales have made.

Finance is managing the cash as it comes into the company and goes out of the company.

Administration is managing the support needed to make sure all of the other departments function efficiently (HR, IT, Front office, Facilities, etc.).

I am in the _____ department.

Next, decide which of the challenges (in the columns) your current position can contribute the most to right now.

I call this concept *start where you are.* Eventually, you may want to reach beyond your department and challenge, but for right now, start where you have the most knowledge and can make the biggest impact.

For example, if you are an accounts payable clerk (in the Finance department), you may choose Increase Efficiency as your challenge. One of the solutions you might think about is to automate the monthly payments that are recurring so that you can focus more on scrutinizing the large, irregular invoices for accuracy.

I will take on this challenge: _____

_____

Once you've located yourself on the grid (both department and challenge), think about the types of problems you could solve using these ideas as a starting point. The topics in the quadrants are typical areas that are highly valuable to growing companies.

Choose one of these ideas (or one of your own), and specifically observe ways that you could solve an issue that would affect this one challenge in your department.

The Start Where You Are Matrix

	Increase sales	Decrease costs	Increase efficiency	Decrease waste
Marketing	Better quality leads What sells? Good, better, best packaging Create demand with content. Run a promotion. Offer free education or speak to target market groups.	Create digital materials vs. printed. Move this in-house or outsource it.	Automate follow up. Tighten up the target market. Narrow your focus. Spend more on target market. Cut spending on programs that don't work.	Measure, spend, and reduce where campaigns are not working. Do mini tests with beta groups before spending large amounts on a campaign. Digitize Analyze trade show and sponsorship spending for potential cuts.

Sales	Create new clients.	Minimize travel expenses.	Qualify prospects.	Simplify brochures and leave-behinds.
	Sell new products and services to existing clients.	Find low cost entertainment that matters.	Invest time with ideal clients. Refine the sales process.	Digitize
	Add a product line.	Examine and cut unnecessary memberships.	Automate follow-up. Create or refine the CRM (software to	Examine the trade show spending. Time management
	Nurture referral partners.		track sales process). Mentor	Delegate or automate non-selling
	Internal competitions		the junior salespeople.	activities.
Operations	Upsell to current customers.	Do more with less.	Automate	Quality Control
	Suggest add-ons for popular products.	Order in bulk. Ask for discounts from suppliers.	Train Education systems	Examine the process. Delegate
	Recommend upgrades.		Innovate Create	authority. Examine the
	Communicate current customers' needs to Marketing.		or refine processes. Maximize machine uptime.	schedules. Avoid overtime.
			Specialize	

Finance	Extend credit to customers.	Negotiate fees and pricing with vendors.	Automate	Crosstrain
	Charge fees for financing.	Create and monitor the departmental budgets.	Specialize	Suggest cost cutting to department.
	Extend the terms to customers.		Outsource	Question every expense.
			Add technology.	
	Make it easy to do business with your company.	Give feedback to departments quickly and regularly.	Simplify	
			Train	
	Decrease the paperwork necessary to sell.			
	Simplify			
Administration	Improve first impression of the company (by phone or in person).	Ask for discounts.	Decentralize	Recycle office supplies.
			Centralize	
		Find new vendors.	Simplify	Centralize
	Retain current clients.			Automate
		Strengthen vendor relationships.	Make people's jobs easier.	Outsource
	Add more *wow factor* for clients.		Cut out unnecessary steps to operate within the company.	Keep others working where they are productive.
		Outsource		
	Know the *A* clients.			
			Automate	
	Form relationships.			

You might get excited and really want to start looking for *many* ways to improve, but resist the temptation. When you try to make everything a priority, nothing is a priority. Practice the art of focus. If you are having a hard time choosing one area on which to focus, think to yourself, *What would make the biggest impact on the important numbers in my department?* (Use the Weekly Numbers Microscope Tool!)

My Issue to Solve

After looking at the Departments and Challenges and reviewing the previous tools (including your TALK with your boss), where do you think you could make the biggest impact right now, for the good of the company?

_____

_____

Now that you've chosen an issue to solve, let's get to work finding the right solution.

Tool: The Issues Solving Track™

Now that you have selected your one area that needs improvement, you need to make sure that you are solving it at its root cause. If you don't stop to question what the true issue is, you'll spend lots of time putting bandages on a wound that won't stop bleeding. The Issues Solving Track from EOS, the Entrepreneurial Operating System, which I teach to leadership teams, will help you do this. We'll use the initials IDS: Identify, Discuss, and Solve.

Identify: Your first task is to identify the root cause of the issue. Ask yourself *why* this is happening. Make a list of possible reasons, then select the one that is your best guess. This will not happen immediately. Spend some time observing and really digging for the root cause. This is an ideal topic for your discussions with your boss. "What do you think about...? Would it be a good idea for me to spend time coming up with a solution to this?"

Discuss: Once you have identified the root cause, gather data that is pertinent to the issue and discuss it with other people. What data do they have that you don't? Research, read, and refine your understanding of the issue.

Solve: Finally, come up with a solution for the issue. Run it by several people, including your boss. Ask, "Would it be a good use of my time to work on implementing this solution?"

Sounds simple, right?

Here's another chance for me to shoot straight with you. This is hard work. The three steps above are challenging to master, even for the leadership teams I coach. It is a *simple* process, but it is not easy. Here are a few tips to help you stay on the right track:

Spend more time identifying: A good checkup (to test whether you're doing this right) is to think about the time you are spending in each phase. I've observed that when people spend most of their time in the Identifying section, the Discussion and the Solve sections come relatively easy. (The solution may not be easy, but seeing it is.)

Slow down: Some of the teams I coach like to mow through their issues like a teenager on a riding mower. It feels like you are being very successful when you solve issues like that, but beware, without the upfront thought, most of the time, issues are just being solved with bandages, duct tape, and twine. Slow down and invest in the *right* solution.

Don't avoid the real issue: Being bold enough to call out the real issue is tough for leadership teams. It will be even tougher for you. Be brave, be bold, be humble, and commit to solving real issues instead of ancillary ones.

A Final Word about Solutions

A great solution makes *everyone's* life easier. How can you make life easier for your boss, your coworkers, the customers, and yourself?

If you are the employee that invests hard work into making others' lives easier, you've produced a solution that will keep serving the company for many years. If your solution can stick around, it will still be producing value even when you've moved on, which brings us to one of my favorite words to pair with productivity: *exponential.* How do you make your productivity exponential?

You learn to serve,
in the final compartment of your toolbox...

SERVE

Where you'll learn how to make sure your productivity spreads like wildfire!

I grew up in a *serve others* household. Service was at the core of our family values (and our businesses). My dad's go-to teaching phrase was, "You've got to know how to please people." Mom's was, "I want my children to grow up to be productive members of society."

As I grew, I found personal joy in serving others. I spent thousands of hours volunteering for one cause or another and, at some point, I realized I was not making a dent in the causes I was serving. This thought poked at my brain cells every time I donated to or worked for a charity.

The book *Crazy Good* by Steve Chandler cleared up this issue for me. In the book, Steve makes a distinction between *serving* and *pleasing*. What I discovered was that all my life, I had been *pleasing* people, not *serving* them. Here's an example from Steve's book to illustrate the point.

When I was a desperate alcoholic and I came to your home and you made me a strong drink, you were pleasing me. If, instead, you took me to a Twelve-Step meeting, you were serving me.

So, there is a big difference between serving and pleasing. There's no substitute for true service. Most people who work for a living have a hard time distinguishing between serving and pleasing. And it's no wonder; we are trained from an early age to please our parents, our school teachers, our religious leaders, etc. So, eventually, it's our default reaction to be pleasing to our boss. We flatter our bosses and become *yes-men* or *yes-women*, telling our bosses what we think would please them, not what they need to hear. Serving will be much more valuable to your boss.

In his acclaimed study, "The Iceberg of Ignorance," consultant Sidney Yoshida concluded: "Only 4% of an organization's front line problems are known by top management, 9% are known by middle management, 74% by supervisors and 100% by employees."

THE ICEBERG OF IGNORANCE

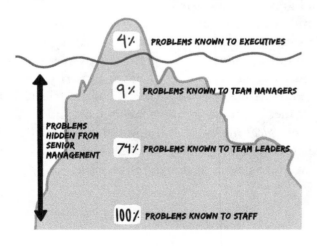

4% PROBLEMS KNOWN TO EXECUTIVES

9% PROBLEMS KNOWN TO TEAM MANAGERS

PROBLEMS HIDDEN FROM SENIOR MANAGEMENT

74% PROBLEMS KNOWN TO TEAM LEADERS

100% PROBLEMS KNOWN TO STAFF

We've already explored how being open and honest will expedite solutions throughout the company. Now, you see how pleasing those around you will only make the "Iceberg of Ignorance" *more* true.

So, how does serving make *you* more productive? It increases your productivity exponentially. The simple definition of exponential is *increasingly rapid* or *very fast*.

Think about it this way: you only have so many hours in your day. At this point, you've found ways to produce more within your eight-hour day, but at some point, you'll hit your maximum. However, if you create an extension of yourself by serving those around you, you'll create more producers, who will also start to produce more, making your efforts multiply *without you there*. Essentially, you'll turn your productivity into rapidly increasing productivity. When your boss sees you as a center of positive influence to your coworkers, you'll become more valuable for your mind *and* your productive output.

Tool: A Go-To Person

Your goal with this tool is to take what you've learned while implementing the previous tools to create more producers (both in performance and energy) around you. When bosses find people like this, sometimes they call them their *go-to* person. This tool will help you become that mentor they are looking for.

You know what it means to serve versus to please, but there is another ingredient in becoming the go-to person in your company and being valued for creating more productivity. It's the difference between being a deficit thinker and a possibility thinker.

Deficit Thinkers are people who think other people will have a hard time learning a new task. They see more issues than solutions. They think the glass is half empty. The world is full of deficits, never good enough. Deficit thinkers are afraid of failure. Think of someone you know who is a deficit thinker.

Possibility Thinkers are people who think that people can learn what they want to learn. They see hope in those around them. They see solutions more than barriers. They think the glass is half full. The world is full of possibility. They are excited for additional growth. Possibility thinkers look at failure as a way to learn. Think of someone who is a possibility thinker.

When we compare serving or pleasing to deficit or possibility thinking, four types of mentors appear. Review these quadrants and see if you recognize yourself or your boss anywhere:

The Four Types of Go-To People

I Serve	**The Professor Approach** "You can't do it so I'll show/tell you how." You create a following of worshipers but can't remove yourself from their productivity. People often comment that they *don't know how you do it.* You are happy to keep your secrets to yourself. You think it brings you job security. Pretty soon, it brings so much security that you get *passed over* for promotions because you can't be replaced. Your influence is limited to your specific knowledge base.	**The Coach Approach** "I remember when I first encountered that issue. Let's think it through together! Now, what have you tried? What else?" You spend more time upfront with people around you and give them opportunities to come up with solutions because you listen more than you talk. You ask good questions to help them think of new ways to look at the situation. You create a team of thinkers around you that eventually creates additional thinkers. You are the center of a giant ripple of productivity.
I Please	**The Buddy Approach** "You can't do it so I'll do it for you." You help but do so begrudgingly. The team is appreciative but asks you to help as a last resort. You end up working harder than anyone else but don't create additional productivity around you. Your only choice to is to work harder or longer.	**The Cheerleader Approach** "You can do it—just try!" Team members love to be around you for your positive motivation, but you rarely create additional productivity. Sometimes, you create messes as a result of your encouragement with no direction or instruction. Pretty soon, people realize they can't go to you with real issues.
	Deficit Thinker	**Possibility Thinker**

When people ask for my help, I am a _____

In order to create Exponential Productivity and become the most productive go-to person in my company, I need to be a _____.

HINT: Using the Coach Approach is the answer! (I guess that wasn't much of a hint!)

Tool: Use the Coach Approach

You don't need to have an official title to be a leader or a coach. Here's how to do it in the most productive way.

Mentor the Puppies—Look for and identify the Puppies in your department and let them know you'd be happy to mentor them. Use this framework to create additional producers around you.

Train—Make sure the puppy has had the right training. Ask good questions like, "Did you read the manual? Have you had training on that machine? What kind of training did you get? Have you had this class yet?" Everyone who is learning a new task/skill deserves to have received the textbook or school-like training needed to do their job. The next three steps are very difficult and take a long time, resulting in a lot of errors if you skip the basic training phase.

Coach—Next, once the training is complete, the puppy will encounter situations where there was a gap in the training, they forgot the training, or they have a special situation. They will come to you if you've made yourself available. Most likely, you'll enter this coaching phase when a puppy asks you a question. Let's say they come to you and say, "Hey, Joan, what button do I push next, the red one or the green one?" If you were raised to be a people-pleaser like me, you'll want to immediately give John the answer, but coaches don't give the puppy the answer. Instead, they start down a humble path of questioning. It might sound like this:

> *Oh, John, I remember when I was just learning on that machine, too. I had some of the same experiences. Tell me, what do you think would happen if you pushed the red button? How about the green? What happened last time you did that? What's the real issue here? What else? What might go wrong? Where else have you looked for your answer?*

Continuing on with this line of questioning gets John's mind to slow down and think. Getting *every* mind on the team in the habit of thinking is the goal when striving to get to exponential productivity.

During this coaching (questions, mostly), Joan and John are going to come up with a solution. Now it's time to implement the solution!

Don't Rescue—The coach does not rescue the puppy. Rescuing looks like this:

> *Hey John, that's a great idea, but this time, the client/project is too important to have a mistake so let me push that red button for you. Or, You're so new and you've never done this before, so just this once, I'll take care of it. Or, This is really tricky/hard, I'll do it for you.*

When you rescue, you are essentially saying, "I don't believe in you and your ability to do your job." This chips away at the confidence level of the puppy and takes them farther away from being productive on their own.

The opposite of rescuing looks like this:

Okay, John, sounds like you have a plan, how can I help?

Let John ask for what he needs from you. At this point, give him pointers or ideas on how you've accomplished this task in the past. If John is nervous (or if you're nervous), offer to sit *with* him as he pushes the red button, hold his hand, be in the room, watch over his shoulder...whatever he needs to be comfortable, but do not do it *for* him. Rescuing does not produce exponential productivity.

Return and Reflect—The last step, and the one that is most overlooked, is the "reflect." Essentially, ask the puppy:

How did it go? What did you learn? What would you do differently next time?

The reason that Return and Reflect works so well is that *it seals in the learning.*

When we put words to our thoughts, we remember them better. In fact, lots of people (including me) learn best when we talk. Others learn best by writing things down, but if we never slow down to think about what we learned, it has the chance to slip away. Solidify the puppy's learning by asking him or her to verbalize it. This also gives you the chance to reinforce that they are on the right track and to give them more encouragement!

LET'S DO A TOOLBOX INVENTORY!

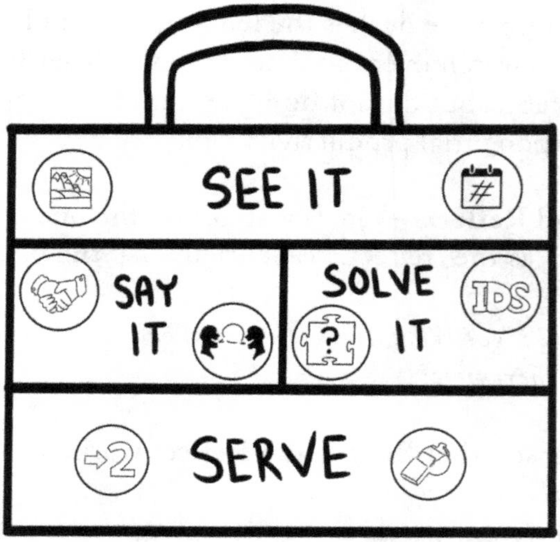

SEE IT
SAY IT
SOLVE IT
IDS
SERVE

Now, all of your toolbox compartments are full. You know how to:

See It: See the big picture and the numbers that are important to the business.
Tool: Big Picture Boot Camp
Tool: Weekly Numbers Microscope

Say It: Have the right conversations with your boss.
Tool: Same Team
Tool: TALK

Solve It: Having observed, you've chosen something to focus on and can move forward with a solution.

    Tool: Where's My Puzzle Piece?

    Tool: Issues Solving Track™

Serve: Create exponential productivity by serving those with whom you work.

    Tool: A Go-To Person

    Tool: Use the Coach Approach

MY INVITATION TO YOU

You know you're a leader when you've created another leader who can create another leader.

We're not quite done here. Remember back to the first few pages when I asked you to be selfish? Well, it's my turn! If you made it through this book and you are experiencing success with these tools, you probably have what it takes to be a leader and a manager in this company. The world of capitalism needs more leaders and managers with your new ability to use the Coach Approach. So, I'm issuing a public, passionate plea for you to consider leadership in your career path. (It's just short of begging...I know.)

Not everyone *wants* to be a leader, or in management, so it will be another journey of exploration you'll take, and you'll ask yourself if leadership is for you, and while you do, consider this thought by the great Seth Godin from his book *Tribes*:

> *Leadership is scarce because few people are willing to go through the discomfort required to lead. This scarcity makes leadership valuable....*
>
> *It's uncomfortable to propose an idea that might fail.*
>
> *It's uncomfortable to challenge the status quo.*
>
> *It's uncomfortable to resist the urge to settle.*

When you identify the discomfort, you've found the place where a leader is needed.

If you're not uncomfortable in your work as a leader, it's almost certain you're not reaching your potential as a leader.

Look at Seth's statement in a different way, paired with what we've already done with the Earning Advantage Toolbox.

What Seth says:	What the Earning Advantage Tools did for you:
"Leadership is scarce because few people are willing to go through the **discomfort** required to lead. This **scarcity** makes leadership valuable. It's uncomfortable to propose an idea that might fail."	If you are using the tools I just gave you, you are probably experiencing some discomfort. Your boss is handing several people in your company this book. Will you be the one to follow through? (4 out of 5 won't or will try then give up). If you're the one that keeps it up, this means you are among the **scarce**.
"It's uncomfortable to **challenge the status quo.**"	If you've been *serving* as I've taught you to, you've **challenged the status quo.**
"It's uncomfortable to **resist the urge to settle.**"	If you've followed through with that second TALK meeting with your boss, you've **resisted the urge to settle.**
"When you identify the discomfort, you've **found the place where a leader is needed**. If you're not uncomfortable in your work as a leader, it's almost certain you're not reaching your potential as a leader."	When you've identified the root cause of a problem, **you've identified where a leader is needed.**

I hope you can see that you're well on your way to becoming the leader your company and our country needs. I'm thrilled to see what your next step will be.

Time to make a toast (grab a beer, a glass of wine, a glass of milk, or some Oreos)

...to your exponential productivity!

APPENDICES

Appendix A
Assessments!

If you are stuck in the land of *What should I do?*, that sucks; no one should stay there for long. It's been my experience that assessments can often help you get *unstuck*. The results of the assessment can help point you in the right direction and create a self-awareness that was not there before. My favorites are:

Culture Index: This survey uses predictive analytics to ensure maximum optimization for yourself and your organization. Being the *right person in the right seat* is essential if you are to apply the Earning Advantage tools personally and professionally. You can email my personal Culture Index advisor, Michael Hall, at Mhall@cindexinc.com, or contact Culture Index directly at www.cultureindex.com. They will email you a free assessment and in less than six-seven minutes, you can get even more insight into your Earning Advantage journey.

Kolbe: This assessment explains how you naturally get things done. It will help you understand how you act, react, and interact and also guide you to job tasks that you'll naturally excel in. You can take the Kolbe A assessment online for about $50.00 at www.kolbe.com.

StrengthsFinder: This assessment helps you identify where your strengths are as a human. You'll apply them in different ways and in different situations. It can help unravel the question of *why* you do what you do and how to use your strengths to do it better. You can take this assessment online for $15.00 at www.gallupstrengthscenter.com.

Appendix B
Sample Written Plan and Template

Thanks again for meeting with me today, _____. Here's a summary of what we talked about.

To be on the path of making more money in the company, the best use of my time would be to:

1.

2.

3.

We also agreed that I can help the department by finding ways to solve the following:

1.

2.

3.

You asked me to mentor _____.
I look forward to meeting again about this in a few weeks.

ACKNOWLEDGMENTS

This book had many champions. Their daily coaching and inspiration pushed me to continue when I was ready to pull my hair out. Thanks team!

My family: Thanks for your support in giving me time to put my energy into this work. It was truly a gift.

My former bosses: Jenny Oakeson, Kathleen Gage, Steve Williams, my mom, and my sister, Joan. Thank you for allowing me to learn under your wing.

My coaches: Thank you for letting me talk through my ideas and my passions, validating my purpose, and redirecting my *crazy!* #honeybadgers

My clients: Thank you for the honor of serving you. Thank you for trusting me to guide you in your growth. You push me to be better every day. Let's never stop growing together.

My advisors: Leslie Horn with Keen Editing Service: You made this fun and efficient. I'll never publish another word without you! Victoria Cabot with Velocity 6: You make genius look effortless. Your brain is amazing! And of course, my right-hand woman, Lindsey: You keep me organized, efficient, and working in my unique ability. If I could only clone you.

My Generation Z workers: At the age of only 15, these young women took on the work of seasoned professional adults and *rocked it.* Audrey Horn: for listening to me babble through book cover ideas and producing more than I thought was possible. Riley Turner: for the graphics in the book. Your ability to take a vision and turn it into a finished product astounded me.

The incredibly smart and efficient team at Author Academy Elite: You took the first edition of this book and made it stronger and readily available to the world to help me fulfill my purpose of inspiring millions!

The team at EOS Worldwide, LLC. The foundation you gave me in EOS has been life-changing. Thank you for pouring into me and believing in my ability to help *you* make a big dent in the universe...to 100,000.

Thank you to my test readers and contributors for your stories and feedback:

Brandon Bachlik, Randy Barber, Chuck Boggess, Tom Bouwer, Walt Brown, John Bryant, Victoria Cabot, Mark Cannon, Steve Chandler, Bill Chinners, Dacia Coffey, Ken DeWitt, CJ Dube, Heather Ettinger, Julie Fleming, Alex Freytag, Ashley Germany, Jessica Glover, Chris Goade, Michael Hall, Mark Halvorson, Drew Hinrichs, Dennis Howard, Glen Katlein, Duane Marshall, Shawn McBride, Joseph Ndesandjo, Rick Pietrykowski, Ron Pyke, Elinor Rowan, Jerry Russell, Roger Sage, Matt Schuval, Jim Suss, Chris White, Gino Wickman, Brandon Young, and James Young.

COURSES

The Earning Advantage Course for Employees

Engage in this deep dive to discover your own personal earning power!

In this 6-week online course, I'll coach you through a series of videos, quizzes, and reflections. You'll graduate from the course as a confident producer with the skills you need to be an earner in both your current and future jobs!

The Earning Advantage Course—Boss Edition

If you are a boss who regularly hands this book to your employees when they ask for a raise, use this course to learn how to:

- coach a high-potential employee
- motivate star performers
- encourage your low performers to find the joy of productivity

If your employees don't currently have the Earning Advantage mindset, the concepts you'll learn in this course are your best chance to get them there!

Visit JillYoung.com to sign up today.

The Earning Advantage

WORKSHOP

Introduce everyone in your company to The Earning Advantage Mindset.

In this interactive workshop, you'll discover:

- » how productivity affects the engagement levels of the company
- » how to identify productivity killers
- » how to offer resources that will help employees understand how they contribute to the company.

The workshop will encourage participants to develop a deeper commitment to serving others so all team members can work toward the organization's success.

INTERACTIVE WORKSHOP: 2-4 HOURS

LIVE KEYNOTE: 60-90 MINUTES

Visit JillYoung.com to sign up your team today!

ACCOUNTABILITY ACTIVATOR

This is a day-long workshop for company leaders in growth mode.

During this workshop, we will explore the mindsets it takes to be a boss who creates an accountable culture. After participating in the workshop, managers will feel confident in their ability to activate the productivity

» on their team

» in their department

» or for the entire company

Designed strictly for management, this session can be held with multiple companies in attendance, or it can be customized for individual organizations.

INTERACTIVE WORKSHOP: 5-7 HOURS

LIVE KEYNOTE: 60-90 MINUTES

Visit JillYoung.com to sign up your leaders today!

EOS
IMPLEMENTATION

Will the Entrepreneurial Operating System (EOS) work for you? Consider these questions:

- » Is the company hitting the ceiling?
- » Is the company changing direction often?
- » Do you get one answer from one manager and a different response from another manager?
- » Could the company benefit from more accountability and discipline?
- » Could the company be more cohesive, open, and honest?
- » Does the owner or leadership team want to improve?

If any of these questions resonate with you, contact me at Jill@JillYoung.com

OTHER BOOKS
BY JILL YOUNG

The Courage Advantage:

3 Mindsets Your Team Needs to Cultivate Fierce Discipline, Incredible Fun, and a Culture of Experimentation

The Thinking Advantage:

4 Essential Steps Your Team Needs to Cultivate Collaboration, Leverage Creative Problem-Solving, and Enjoy Exponential Growth

JILL YOUNG

CPSIA information can be obtained
at www.ICGtesting.com
Printed in the USA
BVHW070442081021
618416BV00003B/8